A Landscape With Birds

First published 2022 by The Hedgehog Poetry Press

Published in the UK by
The Hedgehog Poetry Press
5, Coppack House
Churchill Avenue
Clevedon
BS21 6QW

www.hedgehogpress.co.uk

ISBN: 978-1-913499-95-2

9 8 7 6 5 4 3 2 1

A CIP Catalogue record for this book is available from the British Library.

A Landscape With Birds

Beth Brooke

Contents

JACKDAWS

with
their platinum-bead eyes and that

*"what the fuck do you think
you're looking at?"* expression

have no regard
for the sensibilities of people who

only put out bird feeders
to attract blue tits and chaffinches;

they just turn up and trash the place,
knowing that even though you claim to be

mad at them for gate-crashing your
garden party, you won't shoo them away

because their black feathers are sleek
and speak to you of Parisian punk -

a look that not just any bird can pull off -
I mean, have you checked out a *rook* lately?

Jackdaws know that if you could be a bird,
they are exactly the one that you would want to be.

AUTUMN PANTOUM

Crane flies gather in sinister clusters,
they hang off the walls, refusing to fly
and summer has nothing left, it musters
only purple berries against a fierce blue sky.

They hang off the walls, refusing to fly,
while the swallows slice through the air like knives,
only purple berries against a fierce blue sky
remind us of our summer lives.

While swallows slice through the air like knives,
the opulence of the orchard plums
reminds us of our summer lives
and in the hives of the meadow, the bees hum.

The opulence of the orchard plums,
the parting gift of summer sun
and in the hives of the meadow, the bees hum
the song of a harvest all but done.

The parting gift of summer sun
as the season cools and the shadows creep
the song of a harvest all but done
becomes the lullaby to winter's sleep.

As the season cools and the shadows creep
and summer has nothing left, it musters,
becomes the lullaby to winter's sleep,
crane flies gather in sinister clusters.

WE TAKE OUR SON TO UNIVERSITY

We feel the rhythm of the road; the keening of the wheels
plays upon the skin.

The morning is everything October can be - a liquid brightness
so clear and sharp it cuts; its beauty pains the eyes.

The sky is cloudless;
above the lines of the fields the red kite wheels, slices
through the air, an effortless moving away from us.

The road signs
mark our progress, like the counting down to the moment of launch.

Ten miles left,
conversation stalls as the power station's cooling towers come into view,
scab on the horizon of an otherwise perfect landscape.

We fall to
unfamiliar silence as the slip road drags us to the end point
and like the red kite, you lift off and soar away.

WINTER QUARANTINE

I have taken to sleeping in the attic room.
Hidden under the eaves,
it is the right size to be comforting.
In the lethargy of a winter morning
with its slow summoning of light,
I wake and lie there.

I listen to the rasp of the magpie,
hear the jackdaws argue.
I think about the hedgehog
in its little nest, snug under leaves
and summer hay.

Later, I will visit its spot by the garden wall,
lift the roof of the hibernaculum, peer in.

I will watch it breathing,
the rise and fall of its prickled back;
it will not stir.

GEESE FLY OVER THE PORTLAND ROAD

The geese flew today:
a vanguard of winter.
Like a plough turning the soil,
their skein furrowed the sky;
wings plunging through the air,
pulled up and away from me.
Although the sky was still blue,
still streaked with the soft orange
of an early morning sun,
the sight reminded me that
the season of our growing together
is over, and the harvest done.

POSTCARDS

I. Coast Path above Eype

The sea calls us;
you are not here to answer.
Ravens, paired, tumble overhead;
I stand at the edge to watch
the waves crawl;
my thoughts snag on
splinters of silvered light
across the bay.

II. Christchurch Meadow, Oxford

The boathouses are shut, the river empty.
The drizzle of late December threatens
rain and only the most stubborn
romantic would want to walk the path;
I am the only tourist on the river bank today.

III. The Riad Garden, Marrakesh

The evening is soft and warm;
compassionate, it asks no questions.
I watch the moth burst its heart
against the glass of the table light,
consumed by longing for what
it does not know it cannot have.

IV. Hereford Cathedral

Here is the Mappa Mundi - remember it?
The one with Jerusalem at its centre?
It looks to the east for love.
To some it was a chart of navigation,
a treasure map to others;
a simple relic now, maybe
of a journey undertaken years ago.

V. *Symondsbury*

The pine trees have fruited now,
cones load the branches, heap
themselves on the grass.
I am part of the landscape
beyond what used to be your
window, where the raven
calls its hard, clear song.

IN THE WOOD

The wood holds a ruin:
vestigial altar, and a remnant of wall
faith built centuries ago.

Beech trees roof it now, bluebells floor it.
A carved Christ presides, arms outstretched,
invites you to sit among choirs of birdsong.

I bring the ashes here,

place them on the broken altar stones
and go.

The seasons' turns will scatter them,
grain by grain, and set him free.

Foxes will nose the grey heap,
badgers spread the remains, and

Christ will hang there, arms outstretched,
weary, compassionate.

SOME THINGS TAKE A LONG TIME TO DIE.

There is a creature trapped
inside my neighbour's chimney -
a jackdaw maybe.

She tells me there is nothing
she can do to get it out, the
stove plate fused shut.

I stand there in my hallway,
hear its desperate scrambling,
the futile fluttering of wings.

There is nothing I can do
but listen.

I long for it to give up the struggle
but the days pass and intermittent
noises tell me it's alive.

I hate to think of it trapped there
in the small and sooted dark,
thirsty for the sky and clean rain.

INFLUENZA PANDEMIC 1919

A pale rider came over the hill;
her coldness hung in milky breaths
above the warm earth
of our newly ploughed fields.

She moved among us,
tendrils of her hair snaked around us:
hyphae branching through the
promise of the late spring day.

The dogs did not notice.
They gave no warning growls;
instead they lay quiet by the hearth
and dreamed of rabbits.

In the evening, infected
by a heaviness that dragged
our hearts back down to the
darkest days, we retired early,

the crump of artillery,
pulse of gunfire
pounded our memories.
We lay down and our dreams

were full of pictures:
sons choked in seas of mud or
hung on the wires that were all
the earth could grow.

Those who could
chose not to wake again,
preferring their dreams of the
lost children.

We buried the dead.

With the last clod turned,
the crows startled from scavenging,
rose into the air;

a pale rider up on the hill
turned; spurred her horse away.

We wiped the dirt from our hands
and trudged home.

GHOSTS

Over the ridge and down the hill where
butter- yellow, scented gorse still grows,
we follow a path made by sheep and deer.
At the valley bottom we walk
through orchard remnants of
gnarled apple trees to Bushes Barn.

Flint walled, it bears the scars it
gathered in another life; bricks
plug gaps that were once windows.
The thatch is gone. Now corrugated sheets
of iron form the roof, but the tap outside
still offers water; brambles trace
the boundary of the kitchen garden.

We stand and listen, strain to catch
the echoes of footsteps in the yard,
the sweeping of a broom,
run our hands along
the fireplace lintel,
peer into the ruins of the bread oven,
imagine the children who waited,
hungry for the loaf.

Only as we turn to go
do the white wings strike towards us,
silent as though
even the air beneath them held its breath.

VESTIGES

after a visit to Whitcombe Church, Dorset

The pews are gone but flower wreaths
still decorate the window sills.
Remnants of a final autumn festival,
they crumble slowly, bleached by the filtered sun.

Upon the wall in pale tints of ochre
and of the colour of dried blood, strides
Saint Christopher; he carries the child Christ
high upon his shoulders; they have a river to cross.

In dry heaps along the edges of the walls
are the bats' droppings; they pile in the corners
and on the lip of the pulpit carved from an oak
felled five hundred years ago.

The altar remains, the air around it softened into stillness;
shafts of sunlight and shadows preach.

SOMETIMES

Sometimes I think,
this is all I wanted:
this view from the ridge,
this summer blue,
this ripening harvest;
this light,
filtered through
beech leaves;
the sound of the breeze .

Other times,
there can only be
the rumble of the sea
on shingle,
the salt smell of morning;
the long climb down
from Golden Cap
to Seatown, and me
thinking, *yes, this is*
everything, this is
everything I wanted.

Then there is now,
when I look up into
the sapphire morning sky
and see the swifts;
their boomerang wings slice
my heart, and I stand here
thinking, *yes, they are taking*
the summer with them.

BETRAYAL

Like black plastic scraps,
the wind takes them -

ravens - wheeling up
and out until they are
merely an ellipsis
on a page of sky,

a signifier

of thoughts unfinished,

words unsaid.

Silence falls into the spaces
between words,
freezes kindness
until the silence and
the spaces
swallow us up.

Then, I wonder how it is
that in this void, this silence,

this emptiness,

your heart beats still?

UNBURIAL

Their devotions are meticulous,
from the excision of turf reserved

for post-dig restoration,
to the ceremonial scrape of

archeological trowels -
rhythmic unpicking

of chalk and flint and earth.
The stained soil is holy,

venerated by a tender
brushing away, grain by

grain, until bones emerge:
femur, rib cage, tibia,

skull wearing the startled
expression of the long dead.

Reverently
he is disinterred,

taken with the grave goods
to be placed safe behind glass.

ROBINS: AN ALTERNATIVE ENCYCLOPAEDIA ENTRY

The robin is seen as martial,
disputatious.
It has a reputation for belligerence,
being able to spark an argument
in an empty tree.

A plainsong ticking
asserts its right of occupancy,
communicates a simple message:
Off   Off   Off   Off.
Its more melodic songs are
variations on a single theme,
which may be summarised
as invitations to *have a go -*
if you think you're hard enough.

Yet when evening comes
these birds are slow to roost.
In the dark they are small,
their dreams uneasy,
troubled by visions
of jabbing beaks and the
fierce beating of wings
in landscapes where night is
always cat -shadow black.

THE BEES OF NOTRE DAME

On the roof of the cathedral,
the bees sleep,
soothed by warmth,
by smoke as rich as frankincense;
their dreams hum
with the sweetness of nectar
gathered on the Rive Gauche.
The wax cells soften in the hives;
honey seeps, drips down
unseen, unnoticed, but
the bees sleep.
The crackling far below
drifts into their dreaming
as the rustle of paper wings.

On the pavement
people swarm, drawn by
a memory of faith,
and grief.
They gaze up,
incredulous.

A MORNING WRITING

in the kitchen

dishes are unwashed,
lumpy remnants
of breakfast porridge congeal
unnoticed
in the pan;

the tea, un-drunk, is cold

outside

jackdaws squabble
at the bird feeder;
the sky is a fierce winter shade
of sapphire blue,

cloudless.

She sits in the basement room,
her world shrunk
to the size of her desk,
the silence in her head
makes her jaw ache.

She will not feed the birds
today

FORTUNE TELLER

The magpie is caged,
it does not sing
but crak-crak, crak- crak,
calls out its rage:
staccato bullets
from a rapid-fire gun.

The magpie is caged,
it does not sing,
but crak-crak,
crak-crak,
believes its single state
is prophecy:
                    one for sorrow

this is the fortune
it gives to you
in black and white.

The magpie is caged,
but crak-crak,
crak-crak,
admire the beauty of its wings,
purple shimmers in a slant of sun
they dazzle the eye,
until the future depends
on seeing them fly.

Open the cage,
crak-crak,
crak-crak,

staccato call,
staccato
stabbing beak:
                    one for sorrow.

FINDING THE WING

Will the bird come back for his wing? he asks
as his blue eyes pool with apprehension.
Will its mummy fix it back so it can fly?
He crouches there, inspects the bloodied thing,
observes the ball joint, colour of skimmed milk,
the shredded ligaments, torn from their socket,
sees what's been lost is greater than a wing.

Sunshine warms the brown and creamy feathers;
I reach down, take his anxious little fist
to comfort, make a hand of it again.

I watch his face, still rounded by that trace
of infancy, innocent, I had believed,
of these hard truths of mortality.

PLOUGHING, APRIL 2020

Plough turns the soil,
dark, rich, earth
of the flood plain
not the flinty chalk
of Dorset downs.

Gulls follow, cries
drowning the noise of
the tractor's engine
and the roll of its
wheels across the field;
their excitement is
raucous, voluble.

I watch them follow
the farmer's loamy wake
and in that moment
know how much
I miss the sea.

THE KAUAI O'O BIRD BECOMES EXTINCT.

The whole world is singing
whistling, clicking.

It chitters, growls;
dappled places buzz and hum,
with the amazement of being.

Even the desert rattles, crackles
with an abundance of life.

We have stopped listening,
do not think of our voices
as part of the wild song.

What does it matter
that one small bird in a
remnant of forest,
calls for a mate that will
never answer?

IF OUR ISLAND HAD KOOKABURRAS THEY WOULD DEFINITELY BE LAUGHING NOW

The ravens have gone,
asserted their sovereign right
to choose.

If you look you can see them,
black against the cold January sky,
flying east.

Their cries are hoarse,
exultant with relief, as they follow
the river

and if you dare to look
you can see the Tower, already beginning
to crumble.

THEY JUST SING ANYWAY

Sparrows cluster in the unruly mass
of clematis and honeysuckle
bordering the garden.
They sing ebullient songs
much bigger than themselves,
flit about in the ramshackle
canopy, choose not to see
the cat that sits close and
is dangerous: too sleek,
too grounded in its own nature
not to be a threat.
Maybe they think the nondescript
feathers hide them,
maybe they cannot hear
the beauty of their own voices
and how life longs to take
possession of it.
Maybe, they see the cat and
just sing anyway.

.

ACKNOWLEDGEMENTS

We Take Our Son To University (print anthology *Secret Chords,* Folklore Publishing)

Winter Quarantine (*Dodging the Rain*)

The Geese Fly Over The Portland Road (*Barren Magazine*)

Postcards (*The York Literary Review*)

In The Woods (*The Amethyst Review*)

Influenza Pandemic 1919 (*The Cabinet of Heed*)

Ghosts (*The Cabinet of Heed*)

The Bees of Notre Dame (*Obsessed With Pipework*)

Vestiges (*Obsessed With Pipework*)

Autumn Pantoum (*Poetry Bus*)

If Our Island Had Kookaburras (*Dreich Overflow Edition*)

Unburial (*Marble 10*)

They Just Sing Anyway (*Dreich Overflow edition*)

ABOUT BETH BROOKE

Beth Brooke is a retired teacher and education consultant. Before retirement her writing was focused on pedagogy and she wrote collaboratively with a number of colleagues to produce textbooks and teachers' resources for Key Stage English and History, published by John Murray, Hodder and Collins. Born in the Middle East, she spent the bulk of her childhood in Germany and Libya and her experiences there have had a profound influence on her life. Although she now lives in Dorset and loves the Jurassic Coast, she still longs for the desert. Much of her poetry focuses on the interaction between the self and the landscape and how landscape shapes us. She has been published in a variety of journals both online and print, including *The York Literary Review, Poetry Bus* and *Marble.* Her poem, *We Take Our Son To University*, was awarded a very highly commended in the 2021 Folklore Poetry Prize. This poem features in her Hedgehog Press debut collection, *Landscape With Birds.* She has also been published in the Gloucester Poetry Festival's Pandemic Anthology. She is a regular host and performer at her local spoken word venue and has run a number of poetry workshops. Her superpower is the ability to remove ticks from hedgehogs (no, seriously, she can!)